MW00782922

THE NEED FOR
OIL

By Cory Gunderson

VISIT US AT
WWW.ABDOPUB.COM

Published by ABDO & Daughters, an imprint of ABDO Publishing Company, 4940 Viking Drive, Suite 622, Edina, Minnesota 55435.

Printed in the United States.

Edited by: Sheila Rivera
Contributing Editors: Paul Joseph, Chris Schafer
Graphic Design: Arturo Leyva, David Bullen
Cover Design: Castaneda Dunham, Inc.
Photos: Corbis

Library of Congress Cataloging-in-Publication Data

Gunderson, Cory Gideon.
    The need for oil / Cory Gunderson.
        p. cm. -- (World in conflict. The Middle East)
    Summary: Examines the importance of oil, how it is formed and obtained, the dependenc
of industrialized nations on oil, and why it has become a bargaining chip between Middle
Eastern and Western nations.
    Includes bibliographical references and index.
    Contents: An overview of oil -- Who has oil? -- Who needs oil? -- Organization of
Petroleum Exporting Countries (OPEC) -- Middle East conflicts and oil -- The future of oi
    ISBN 1-59197-417-8
        1. Petroleum industry and trade--Political aspects---Middle East--Juvenile literature. 2.
World Politics--21st century--Juvenile literature. [1. Petroleum industry and trade--Middle
East. 2. World politics--21st Century. 3. Middle East--Politics and government--1979-] I.
Title II. World in conflict. Middle East.

    HD9576.M52G86 2003
    338.2'7282--dc21

                                                                    2003044376

TABLE OF CONTENTS

Oil is an essential product in the industrialized world.

AN OVERVIEW OF OIL

Oil is an essential part of our lives. Some have called it the lifeblood of industrialized countries. Oil products are needed not just to fuel the car or bus you may have ridden in today. These products are also used in crayons, bubble gum, eyeglasses, ink, and dishwashing liquids. Oil products are most likely used to control the temperature of your home and school, too. Oil is the largest single source of energy in the world today.

Petroleum is another word for oil. "Petra" means rock, and "oleum" means oil. Put together, petroleum means "rock oil" or "oil from the earth." Experts believe that oil is made up of dead plants and animals that lived in water millions of years ago. Through the years, layers of mud covered what remained of these plants and animals. The combination of heat and pressure turned these remains into crude oil.

Crude oil is a liquid that can range in color from yellow to green or black. This smelly substance is typically found in areas underground, which are called reservoirs. Engineers and scientists examine rock samples from a chosen area. If samples reveal the rocks contain oil, then measurements of the area are taken. Drilling begins when it looks like ample amounts of oil are available in a specific area. A tower-like structure called a derrick is built over the drilled hole. The derrick houses the pipes and tools that go into the hole, which is also called a well. When the derrick is constructed, the drilled well will produce a constant flow of oil from underground to the surface.

Once crude oil is removed from the ground, a ship, barge, or pipeline carries it to a refinery. There the oil is separated into different petroleum products, which are used in our lives every day.

The business of oil production is expensive, complex, and time consuming. Producers spend billions of dollars to explore areas and then build the equipment to pump oil. It can take from three to ten years to locate a drill site and develop it. Except for bad weather and other problems, the oil industry works 24 hours a day, 365 days a year. It is very expensive and difficult to shut down oil production, especially when the site is in the ocean.

The United States uses more oil than any other country in the world. Facts from 2001 showed that the U.S. used almost 20

A Kuwaiti oil refinery at sunset

million barrels of petroleum a day that year. The U.S. cannot produce enough to support its needs.

The Middle East is known for having the world's largest supply of oil. For many years, countries, including the U.S., depended on the Middle East for much of their oil. These countries were hit with extremely high Middle East oil prices in the 1970s. After that, the U.S. government focused on ways to lessen the country's need for Middle East oil. Other nations around the world sought alternatives to oil as well.

Increasingly, oil has become an important bargaining chip between countries. Through the years, some Middle East countries would not sell oil to the Western nations that angered them. Oil sales have been restricted by the United Nations, or UN, to punish some Middle East countries for violations. Wars have been fought, which means people have even died, for oil.

The following chapters explain the business of oil and its role in conflicts. They also describe why countries are so dependent on the smelly, sticky liquid we call oil.

WHO HAS OIL?

Oil producing countries have oil that is in reserves as well as oil they produce. It is important to know that different sources may show either or both of these measurements. Reserve amounts and production amounts for the same country may be quite different. A country may have much oil in its reserves but may not produce much.

When you read about oil reserves, you are learning about estimated amounts of oil. Experts in the oil business make educated guesses as to how much oil they expect can be pumped from existing reservoirs.

The U.S. Energy Information Administration, or EIA, showed that at the end of 2000, the U.S. had about 22 billion barrels in its reserves. That's about four percent of the world's oil reserves. The states with the highest reserve levels included: Texas, Alaska, California, New Mexico, and Oklahoma.

The U.S. produces about half of the petroleum it needs. Texas, Alaska, California, Louisiana, and Oklahoma are the top

OIL RESERVES

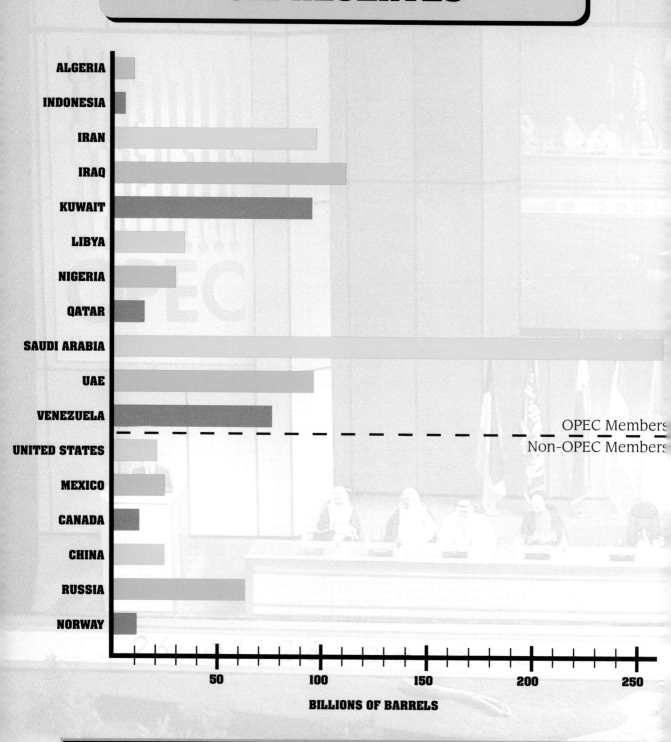

ALGERIA
INDONESIA
IRAN
IRAQ
KUWAIT
LIBYA
NIGERIA
QATAR
SAUDI ARABIA
UAE
VENEZUELA

---- OPEC Members
Non-OPEC Members

UNITED STATES
MEXICO
CANADA
CHINA
RUSSIA
NORWAY

50   100   150   200   250

BILLIONS OF BARRELS

This graph shows the amount of oil reserves held by the 11 members of OPEC and 6 non-members.

Source: OPEC Annual Statistical Bulletin,

OIL PRODUCTION

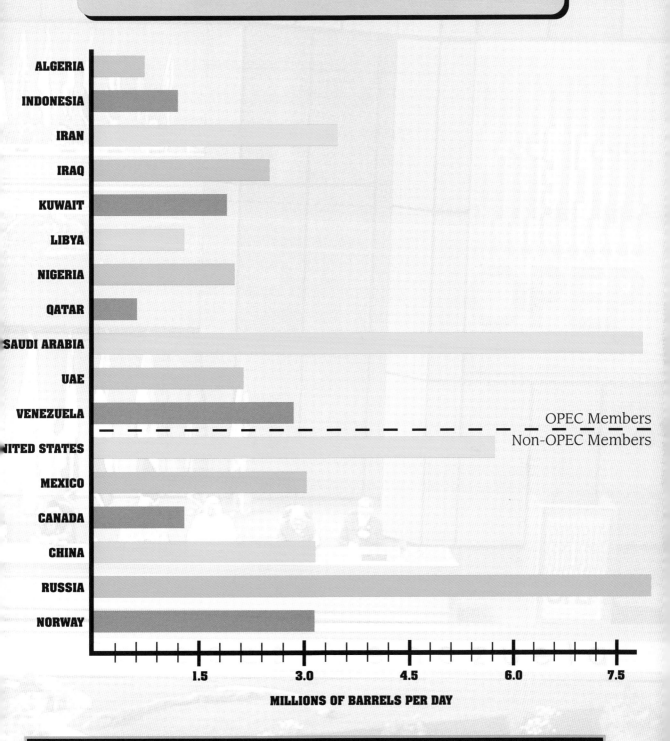

ALGERIA
INDONESIA
IRAN
IRAQ
KUWAIT
LIBYA
NIGERIA
QATAR
SAUDI ARABIA
UAE
VENEZUELA

OPEC Members
Non-OPEC Members

UNITED STATES
MEXICO
CANADA
CHINA
RUSSIA
NORWAY

1.5   3.0   4.5   6.0   7.5

MILLIONS OF BARRELS PER DAY

This graph shows the amount of oil produced by the 11 members of OPEC and 6 non-members.

Source: OPEC Annual Statistical Bulletin, 2001

crude oil-producing states. The U.S. has large deposits of oil and a rich history of producing it. Unfortunately, some U.S. oil fields have been pumping for more than 50 years. This makes them some of the oldest in the world. While there is still oil in U.S. ground, it will be more difficult to get at than the oil pumped earlier. The U.S. spends billions of dollars each year on oil imported from other countries.

The Middle East dominates the world in oil reserves. This region holds more than 65 percent of the world's reserves. The Organization of the Petroleum Exporting Countries, or OPEC, tracks oil information. This organization listed those countries that had the world's largest crude oil reserves in 2001. Saudi Arabia topped the list. It had more than 262 billion barrels in reserve. Iraq had more than 112 billion barrels, and Iran had nearly 100 billion. The United Arab Emirates had almost 98 billion barrels of oil in reserve. Kuwait had about 96 billion.

It is interesting to compare this information to the countries that produce the most oil. According to another 2001 OPEC chart, Saudi Arabia produces close to eight million barrels a day. Russia produces more than eight million barrels daily, and the U.S. close to six million. Iran produces three and a half million barrels daily, and China produces slightly more than three million.

Each region of the world has crude oil. As of 2001, Mexico had the greatest amount of oil reserves in North America. In

Central and South America, Venezuela had the most. China had the greatest amount of oil in Asia. Libya had the most oil reserves in Africa. Although Western Europe does not have much crude oil, Norway had more than its neighboring countries. In Eastern Europe, Russia had the most. No region, though, has more oil than the Middle East.

A worker makes some adjustments at an oil refinery in Iraq.

WHO NEEDS OIL?

People pay attention to oil in terms of how much is in reserves and how much is produced. They also pay attention to consumption rates. These rates tell us how much oil is being used.

When it comes to worldwide consumption rates, the U.S. and Canada currently use far more oil than other nations do. In fact, on a per person basis, these two North American countries together use more oil than the rest of the world combined. In 2001, the U.S. used more than 18 million barrels of oil per day. After North America, Asia and Europe used the most oil. The U.S. and Canada use more oil for transportation than for power and heat. Most other regions of the world use oil for power and heat more than for transportation.

As countries grow economically, their need for oil increases. As industries produce more, they need more energy. More fuel is needed for the trucks that transport what has been produced. Stores and businesses need more energy for lighting, heating, or air conditioning. Then buyers need oil to get to the products they need.

To get an idea of how dependent the U.S. is on oil, consider the number of cars and trucks on the highways each day. Think of how many airplanes and trains transport people and cargo each day. All of these vehicles require oil products to run. Think of all the factories across the country. Each of these depends on oil products to run its machinery. Farmers depend on fertilizer made from oil products to grow their crops. Oil products are probably a part of the plastic jug that holds your milk and the pen you used today. Even your toothbrush is likely made from oil products.

The need for oil has increased faster in poorer countries than in richer ones. Less developed countries depend on manufacturing more than well-developed countries do. In poorer countries, urbanization, or the movement of people from the country to the city, has resulted in increased demands for oil. An increase in car ownership in these countries has had the same effect. In the early 1970s, the demand for oil in developing countries was about 26 percent of the total demand. By the early twenty-first century, their share was close to 40 percent and growing.

OIL CONSUMPTION

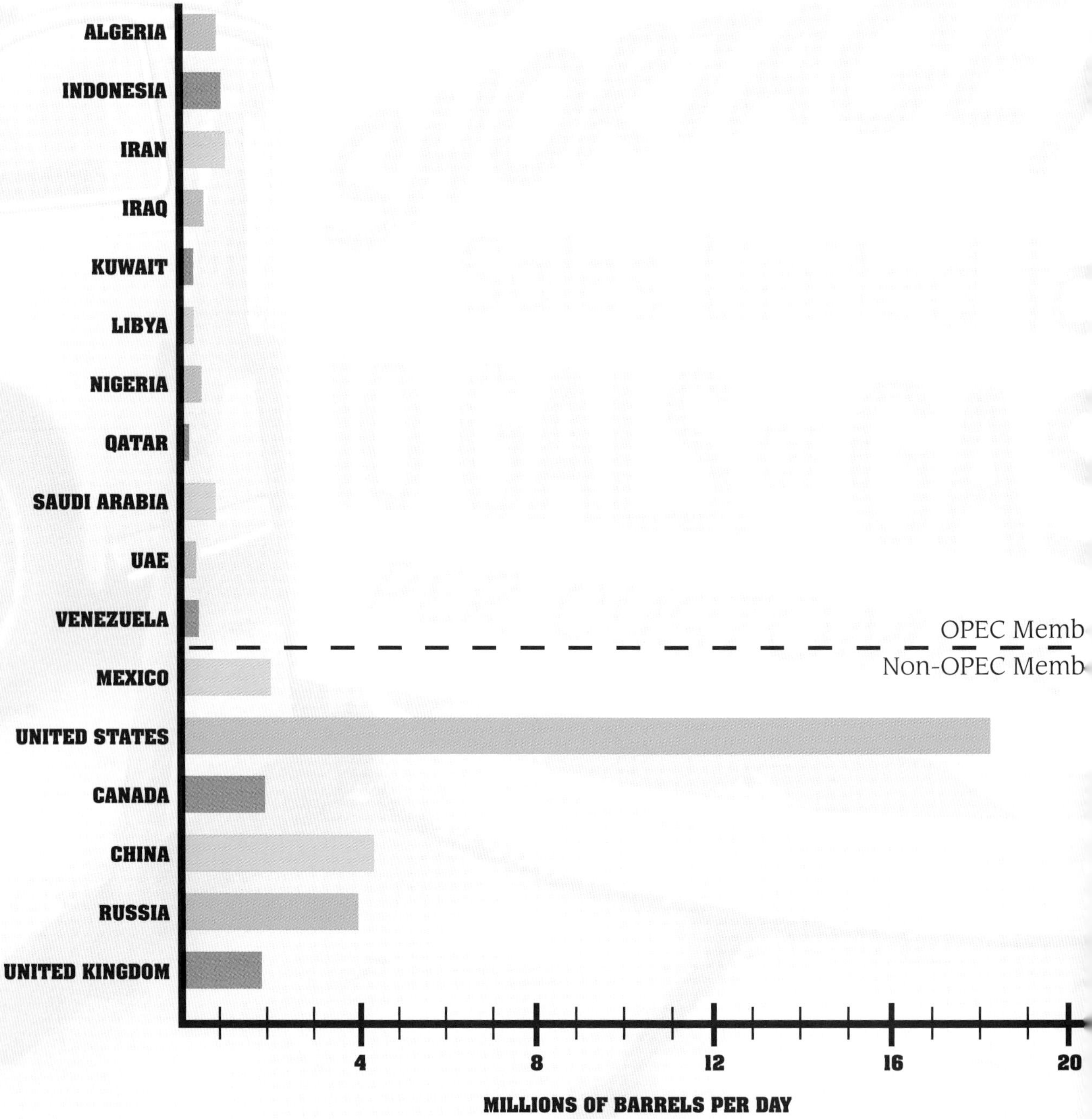
ALGERIA
INDONESIA
IRAN
IRAQ
KUWAIT
LIBYA
NIGERIA
QATAR
SAUDI ARABIA
UAE
VENEZUELA
OPEC Memb
Non-OPEC Memb
MEXICO
UNITED STATES
CANADA
CHINA
RUSSIA
UNITED KINGDOM
4
8
12
16
20
MILLIONS OF BARRELS PER DAY

The U.S. consumes more refined oil products than any other country in the world.

Source: OPEC Annual Statistical B

ORGANIZATION OF PETROLEUM EXPORTING COUNTRIES (OPEC)

F or decades, Western oil companies controlled most of the income that was made from oil produced on foreign lands. Wealthy U.S. families like the Rockefellers and the Gettys once owned some of these oil companies.

Venezuela approached Iran, Iraq, Kuwait, and Saudi Arabia in 1949 with the suggestion that these countries band together. The Venezuelan government felt that oil-producing countries should take more control over how much they earned from the crude oil they sold.

From September 10 to September 14, 1960, Iran, Iraq, Saudi Arabia, Venezuela, and Kuwait met in Baghdad, Iraq. At this First Conference, these oil-producing nations united to protect their oil interests. They formed the Organization of Petroleum Exporting Countries, or OPEC.

Geneva, Switzerland, was OPEC's headquarters for its first five years. In 1965, OPEC headquarters were moved to Vienna, Austria.

OPEC's Conference is the ultimate authority for the organization. This organization operates on the principle of one country, one vote. The Conference is made up of delegations, which are typically led by each country's Oil Minister. The Conference meets at least twice yearly. Its purpose is to draft OPEC policies and then determine how the policies should be implemented. The Conference also decides which applications for membership OPEC will accept.

After each member country decides on its OPEC Governor, it is up to the Conference to approve these choices. Each Governor serves for two years. The Conference also elects the Chairman of the Board.

The Board of Governors manages OPEC's business. It operates like a board of directors does in many non-oil related businesses. The Board implements resolutions to the Conference and proposes its annual budget to the Conference for approval. The Board also forwards reports and makes recommendations to the Conference.

The Secretariat consists of the Secretary General and other required staff. The Secretary General can legally represent

de Septiembre, Caracas-Ve

Representatives from OPEC's 11 member countries

OPEC. He administers the business of OPEC as the Board of Governors has outlined in its policies.

The Research Division is one of several that reports to the Secretary General. Its role is to continuously search for information regarding energy and other related topics. The division watches developments in the energy and petroleum industries. It studies financial and economic issues, especially those related to the world's oil industry. As OPEC collects and studies this information, it helps the organization set its prices.

In 1962, about two years after it was founded, OPEC was formally registered with the UN Secretariat. OPEC's main goals are listed as:

- The coordination and unification of petroleum policies of member countries and the determination of the best means for safeguarding their interests, individually and collectively.
- Finding ways and means of ensuring the stabilization of prices in international oil markets with a view to eliminating harmful and unnecessary fluctuations.
- At all times, protect the interests of the oil producing nations. Secure a steady income for them.
- Provide consuming nations an efficient, economic, and regular supply of petroleum.
- Provide a fair return of their capital to those who invest in the petroleum market.

OPEC wanted to gain power for all member nations by forming a united front. Together, these nations positioned themselves to bargain with the giant oil companies in ways they could not have alone. Their end goal was to keep more oil income for the countries producing it.

OPEC is made up of 11 oil-exporting nations. The majority of countries that currently belong to OPEC are from the Middle East. These members include Iran, Qatar, Saudi Arabia, Iraq, United Arab Emirates, and Kuwait. Qatar became a member in 1961. The United Arab Emirates joined in 1967. The three African OPEC members are Algeria, Libya, and Nigeria. Libya joined in 1962, Algeria in 1969, and Nigeria joined in 1971. Venezuela is OPEC's only South American member. Indonesia is OPEC's only Asian member. It joined in 1962.

In order to become a member of OPEC, a country must sell a minimum amount of crude petroleum. It must also have the same basic interests as the other member countries.

There are three levels of OPEC membership. The three levels are Founder Member, Full Member, and Associate Member. The five countries that attended OPEC's First Conference make up the Founder Members. Full Members are countries that applied to join OPEC and were accepted by 75

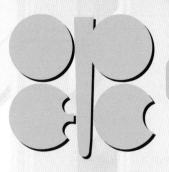

ORGANIZATION OF PETROLEUM EXPORTING COUNTRIES

1960
Iran, Iraq, Saudi Arabia, Venezuela, and Kuwait meet in Baghdad, Iraq, and form OPEC.

1961
Qatar joins OPEC.

1962
OPEC formally registers UN Secretariat.

Libya joins OPEC.

Indonesia joins OPEC.

1965
OPEC headquarters move to Vienna, Austria.

1967
United Arab Emirates joins OPEC.

1969
Algeria joins OPEC.

1971
Nigeria joins OPEC.

1973
Ecuador joins OPEC.

1992
Ecuador leaves OPEC.

VENEZUELA

KUWAIT

IRAQ

SAUDI ARABIA

IRAN

Founder members of OPEC
- - - - - - - - - - - - - - - - - - -
Full members of OPEC

UNITED ARAB EMIRATES

LIBYA

ALGERIA

QATAR

INDONESIA

NIGERIA

percent of full OPEC members. To become a Full Member, a country also has to receive a yes vote by each Founder Member. A country becomes an Associate Member when it does not qualify for Full Member status but is admitted by the Conference under special conditions.

OPEC member countries work to match each other's petroleum policies. The countries may decide to put a limit on the amount of oil each country produces. They can also decide to produce more oil. Together, these nations work to keep oil prices stable and to earn a steady income from oil.

In recent years, OPEC has produced about 41 percent of all the world's crude oil. It has controlled nearly 55 percent of the oil sales between countries. Other large oil producers who do not belong to OPEC, such as Mexico, Russia, and Norway, will sometimes follow OPEC's lead in pricing and policy.

MIDDLE EAST CONFLICTS AND OIL

OPEC didn't have much effect from its beginning in 1960 until the early 1970s. By the early 1970s, the need for Middle Eastern oil was growing in the U.S. and other Western nations. The demand for oil in these industrialized countries grew faster than oil was being produced. The U.S., for example, had been able to produce most of the energy it needed up until the early 1950s. By the early 1970s, the U.S. had to import almost 35 percent of the energy it needed.

Events in the Middle East affected countries around the world that had relied on this region for oil. Three events in particular stand out because of their impact on the countries that bought and sold Middle Eastern oil. The first was the Yom Kippur War in 1973. The second was the Iranian Revolution in the late 1970s. The third event was the Persian Gulf Crisis in the early 1990s.

During the Gulf War, Iraqi troops set Kuwaiti oil fields on fire.

Yom Kippur War

On October 6, 1973, which was Yom Kippur, Egypt and Syria launched a surprise attack on Israel. Yom Kippur is the holiest day on the Jewish calendar. Egypt, Syria, and other Middle Eastern countries resented that the Jews were living on the land once called Palestine. Palestine had been Arab land until the Jewish people claimed it as their homeland. Since the Jewish people declared their independence in 1948, they've called the land Israel.

While the Soviet Union supported the Arab states, the U.S. supported Israel. On October 22, 1973, the UN Security Council adopted a cease-fire resolution.

Arab nations were angered by the U.S.'s support of Israel. They said that they would keep reducing the amount of oil they produced until Israel withdrew from Arab land. In late 1973, the Arab nations drew up an embargo policy. The embargo meant that Arab countries refused to sell oil to the countries that supported Israel.

As part of the embargo, the Arabs divided countries into categories. The first category included the countries that were thought to be friends with Israel. The U.S. and Holland were among the countries in this category. They were not allowed to buy oil from Middle East oil producers. The second category included countries that were labeled exempt. These countries were allowed to buy oil, but in limited quantities. A third category was called non-exempt. Non-exempt countries could divide up and buy whatever oil was left over after exempt countries had bought their shares.

Besides the embargo, OPEC decreased its production of oil. Arab anger also made OPEC countries more determined than ever to get what they felt were fair prices for their oil.

OPEC countries were, for the first time, showing real unity. Together they refused to bargain with oil companies over the price of their oil. This was a turning point in OPEC's history. Western nations realized they were dependent on OPEC oil. Those who could buy OPEC oil paid the price OPEC demanded. The organization had finally held the power it sought. It was finally in control of the world oil market.

OPEC's actions caused oil shortages and the price of oil to increase. The price of oil had jumped from $4 a barrel to about $12 a barrel within six months. In the U.S., cars snaked through gas stations and around the blocks hoping to buy gasoline, which is an oil product. About half a million U.S. jobs were lost in this time. Japan and Western Europe were also hit hard by this embargo and price hikes. The Arab oil embargo was lifted six months after it was imposed.

GAS SHORTAGE! Sales Limited to 10 GALS. OF GAS. PER CUSTOMER

OPEC's oil embargo in the 1970s hit hard in the U.S.

The U.S. government and other governments made efforts to protect their countries from such hardship again. Efforts were made to conserve energy and to switch from petroleum to cheaper fuel choices. One example of these efforts includes work the National Aeronautics and Space Administration, or NASA, did in the 1970s with several universities. This group developed new designs for vehicles, which created fuel savings of 20 to 24 percent. The car industry also used these designs to increase how far cars could travel on a gallon of gas. The creation of the compact car resulted.

In 1974, the U.S. government joined with 20 other countries to form the International Energy Agency, or IEA. Members of the IEA developed plans to store large supplies of oil in case of future shortages or huge price increases. Laws and policies were also made over the next several years that protected U.S. interests and impacted most phases of the oil industry.

Iranian Revolution of 1978–1979

The Iranian Revolution began in late 1978. In January 1979, Shah Mohammad Reza Pahlavi left Iran against his will. The Shah was Iran's leader for decades and a friend of the U.S. government. He had been removed from power by Islamic extremists who were under the guidance of Ayatollah Ruholla Khomeini.

The revolution was the result of an enduring conflict within Iran. The Shah of Iran and his supporters were on one side of the conflict. This group had a close relationship with the U.S. government. Members of this group were building a modern society with the money they made from selling oil. They were protected by military equipment they received from Western nations.

On the other side of the conflict was Khomeini, an Islamic extremist, and his followers. They hated the Western influence that went against Islamic law. They resented and resisted the changes that the Shah and his followers had implemented.

Oil importers were worried that Iran's unrest could lead to disturbances in the world's oil supplies. The instability of the Iranian government led to rising oil prices. Leaders of Western nations and other nations dependent on foreign oil met in Tokyo in June 1979. Instead of competing for oil like they once did, these governments banded together. They planned to deal proactively with OPEC's oil price increases and reductions in supplies. They agreed to cut imported oil by certain amounts. They pledged to work together to use more coal and to develop other energy sources.

رهبر انقلاب:

آمریکا شیطان

بزرگ است.

U.S. IS THE

REAT SATAN

DOWN WITH U.S.A

Iranian women demonstrate the ideals of the Iranian Revolution.

From 1978 until 1981, Iran's crude oil production dropped. Between 1979 and 1981, OPEC crude oil prices rose higher than ever before. By 1981, OPEC's production of crude oil declined by seven million barrels per day from 1978 levels.

While OPEC was cutting back on oil production, non-OPEC governments began to build reserve supplies. Worldwide crude oil prices rose from about $14 a barrel in early 1979 to over $35 a barrel in early 1981. Not until 1983 did prices stabilize at $28 to $29 a barrel.

OPEC's high oil prices prompted governments to explore and then produce oil in non-OPEC countries. Older non-OPEC wells were pumped for longer than they would have been otherwise. The development of oil fields in Mexico, Alaska, and the North Sea resulted in healthy increases to the world's oil supplies.

Also during this time of high oil prices, different types of fuel were being used instead of oil. Household machines, business equipment, and motors were designed to use less oil. These conservation efforts took place in the U.S. and around the world. The demand for oil worldwide fell about five percent from 1980 until 1985.

Throughout the 1980s, some OPEC countries cheated on their production quotas. Each OPEC country had agreed to produce and sell only a certain amount of oil to non-OPEC countries. When an OPEC country sold more than it was supposed to, it hurt all OPEC members. It weakened the organization's ability to bargain with countries that needed their oil.

Persian Gulf War

Iraq invaded Kuwait on August 2, 1990. Iraqi leader Saddam Hussein claimed that Kuwait had cheated OPEC by producing more oil than it had agreed to produce. Saddam was also angry that Kuwait hadn't forgiven the money Iraq owed the country. The two sides also argued about ownership of an oil reservoir. This reservoir, called the Rumaila oil field, lay beneath both sides of the shared Iraqi-Kuwaiti border. Both sides had pumped oil from the field at different times. Iraq accused Kuwait of draining the field.

Crude oil prices rose quickly. The UN called for an embargo on oil coming from both Iraq and Kuwait. The price of oil increased to $36 a barrel by September of that year. In October, the UN approved the use of force against the invading Iraqi military. Oil prices fell.

The U.S. military and its allies stormed into Kuwait in early 1991. The U.S. goal was to drive Iraq out of Kuwait.

The U.S. Army heads to Iraq as Kuwaiti oil fields burn in the background.

The U.S. also wanted to protect its oil interests in Kuwait. This invasion, lasting less than two months, was called the Persian Gulf War.

Saudi Arabia, the most productive OPEC oil producing country, was also the highest producer in the world. It agreed to raise its oil production to compensate for the loss of sales from Iraq and Kuwait. The U.S. agreed to protect Saudi Arabia with its military. Venezuela, the United Arab Emirates, and other OPEC nations followed Saudi Arabia's lead. Iraq threatened these OPEC nations for producing extra oil.

THE FUTURE OF OIL

The U.S. involvement in the Persian Gulf War showed that the nation clearly understood the importance of Middle East oil. The U.S. government went to war to protect the oil that is so necessary to its citizens' way of life.

The security of the U.S.'s energy supply seems to rest upon what happens in the Middle East. After the Persian Gulf War, the relationship between Saudi Arabia and the U.S. became stronger than ever. The U.S. needs Saudi oil, and the Saudis benefit by doing business with the U.S.

Unity among OPEC countries has not always been dependable. While OPEC members saw the power that could result from banding together, differences may separate them. Within OPEC, there are two different mindsets. The first mindset, which includes countries like Saudi Arabia, seeks to keep oil prices moderate. The second mindset, which includes

A Middle Eastern oil refinery

countries like Libya, wants higher oil prices than seem reasonable to oil buyers.

Those OPEC countries that cheat on production quotas also threaten OPEC as an organization. Even though OPEC has existed for more than 30 years, the organization has not been good about enforcing its policies.

Even with all of OPEC's issues, the importance of Middle East oil remains clear. If the organization's member countries repeat the cooperation they demonstrated in the early 1970s, they will continue to dominate the world's oil supplies. If they cannot repeat this success, oil supplies and prices will continue to fluctuate unpredictably.

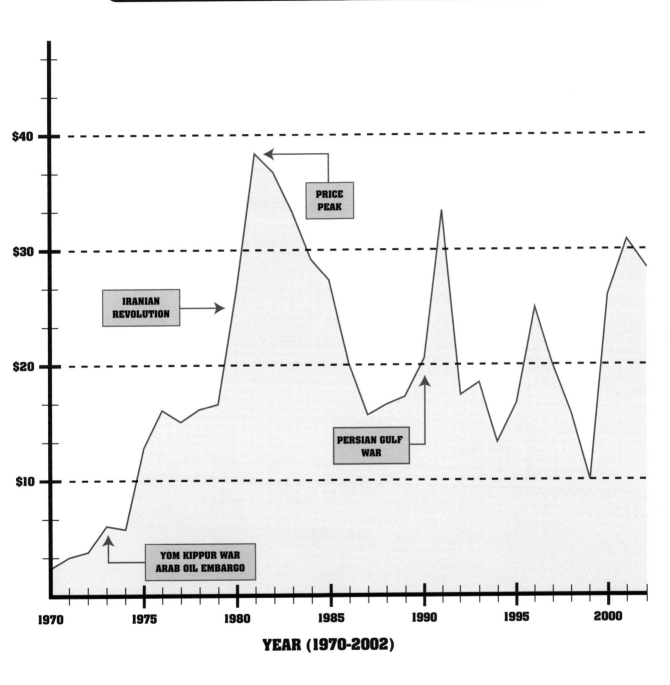

CRUDE OIL PRICES

$40

$30

IRANIAN
REVOLUTION

PRICE
PEAK

$20

PERSIAN GULF
WAR

$10

YOM KIPPUR WAR
ARAB OIL EMBARGO

1970   1975   1980   1985   1990   1995   2000

YEAR (1970-2002)

Middle East events can interrupt the oil supply and cause fluctuations in oil prices.

Source: Energy Information Administration, 2002
Prices do not reflect inflation

OPEC Secretary General Ali Rodriquez of Venezuela

TIMELINE

1949	Venezuela approaches Iran, Iraq, Kuwait, and Saudi Arabia to suggest the five countries should band together to better control their oil earnings.
1960	Iran, Iraq, Saudi Arabia, Kuwait, and Venezuela meet in Baghdad, Iraq, from September 10 to September 14. This is OPEC's First Conference.
1965	OPEC's headquarters move from Geneva, Switzerland, to Vienna, Austria.
1973-1974	A turning point in OPEC history. OPEC gains control of the world oil market.
1974	International Energy Agency (IEA) is formed to protect the oil interests of non-OPEC countries.
1979	The Iranian Revolution causes a change in the country's leadership and changes the U.S.'s relationship with Iran.
1990	Iraq invades Kuwait on August 2. This triggers the Persian Gulf War.
2003	The possibility of a war between Iraq and the U.S. and its allies causes gas prices to increase.

FAST FACTS

- The word "petroleum" means "rock oil" or "oil from the earth." Oil is another word for petroleum.

- Oil is the world's single most important source of energy. It is used more than any other form of energy.

- OPEC was founded in 1960 but didn't gain control of the world's oil market until the early 1970s.

- A 42-gallon barrel of crude oil produces just over 44 gallons of petroleum products. Its volume increases as it is processed.

- Saudi Arabia has typically been the top crude oil-producing country in the world.

- Texas is the top crude oil-producing state in the U.S.

- As of 2001, the U.S. petroleum consumption rate was almost 20 million barrels a day.

- In recent years, the U.S. and Canada used more oil per person than the rest of the world combined.

- The amount of crude oil produced in the U.S. has been decreasing every year.

- NASA has designed ways to make vehicles more fuel efficient. According to this organization, if all U.S. vans and box-shaped trucks followed NASA's design suggestions, 26 million barrels of fuel would be saved per year. This amount of saved fuel would allow about 1.3 million cars to all drive once around the world.

- According to OPEC, its oil reserves should last another 80 years if we continue to use oil at the same rates we do now. The oil reserves of non-OPEC producers might last less than 20 years. OPEC advises that we manage our resources well, use oil efficiently, and continue to develop more oil fields.

GLOSSARY

Baghdad:
The capital and largest city of Iraq, in the center of the country on the Tigris River.

board of directors:
A group of people chosen to manage the business of a corporation.

boycott:
To stop using, buying, or dealing with a person, organization, or country as a form of protest.

cease-fire:
An order to stop fighting.

consumption:
The using up of goods and services by consumers.

coordination:
Planned interaction between two or more parties.

crude oil:
Unrefined petroleum; petroleum in its natural state.

division:
A section of an organization.

embargo:
An order by a government to stop certain or all trade with a foreign nation.

exempt:
To free from a penalty.

fluctuate:
To rise and fall in wave-like motion.

Islamic extremist:

A Muslim who interprets the Koran, or Islamic holy book, strictly.

lifeblood:

A substance that is essential for life.

market (petroleum market):

An exchange for buying and selling oil.

mindset:

A fixed way of thinking.

proactive:

Acting in advance to deal with an expected problem.

refinery:

A factory that purifies a crude substance, such as oil.

revolution:

To overthrow a government and replace it with another.

safeguard:

A measure that protects.

unification:

To make into a unit; to become one.

United Nations (UN):

An international organization made up of most countries of the world. It was founded to promote peace, security, and economic stability.

United Nations Secretariat:

The administrative arm of the United Nations.

violation:

The act of breaking a promise or a law.

Western countries:

Nations in the western hemisphere that typically have high Christian populations.

WEB SITES
WWW.ABDOPUB.COM

Would you like to learn more about The Need for Oil? Please visit www.abdopub.com to find up-to-date Web site links about The Need for Oil and the World in Conflict. These links are routinely monitored and updated to provide the most current information available.

Without oil, there would be no gasoline for cars.

OPEC headquarters in Vienna, Austria

INDEX